Lloyd H. Bell, Jr.

Clean and Serene:

Scriptural Meditations for Recovery

Habakkuk Books, Inc.

Habakkuk Books, Inc. 863 Flat Shoals Rd.
Suite C #174
Conyers, GA  30094
www.Habakkukbooks.com

Printed in the United States of America

First Printing, 2016

Author's Note: This is written in the first person. The term *we* is used often because it has been said that this is a *we* program.  That means this book is written to include all addicts in every phase of the recovery process.  There is still hope, we do recovery.

# In Loving Memory of
# My Cousin Andre Bell.

"This book is dedicated to the still suffering
addict and those in the process of recovery."

*L H Bell*

# PREFACE

This book was written for the sole purpose of helping those who are currently battling or have had struggles with addictions. More specifically this book is meant to be a resource for those in recovery. It can serve as one of the tools in the toolbox of the recovering addict. Having experienced what it means to be caught in the grips of addiction I can relate to the struggle many are facing. I was introduced to addiction and alcoholism as a child when I observed the toll it took on my father and many of my relatives. I was also introduced to the 12 Step Family support groups as a teenager. I would have never guessed at that time that roles would reverse and I would be in need of interventions, support, treatment for alcoholism and other addictions later in life.

My addiction took me further than I wanted to go and kept me longer than I wanted to stay. There were days I had nearly lost all hope of ever getting clean and staying clean. It seemed that I was destined to continue the cycle of addiction and relapse. Many times, I attempted to stop. Like others suffering from this sickness, I found myself in jails and institutions due to my addiction. I tried counseling, support groups and treatment programs of all types, both long and short term, inpatient and outpatient. Family members began to wonder if I would ever get myself together. My story is not unlike the stories of many others who have, by the Grace of God, survived addiction and have begun the wonderful process of healing and recovery. Many people in recovery know the slogan, "Don't give up five minutes before the miracle." (Author unknown). Plain and simple, my message is hope. We do recover!

During my active years of addiction there were three components that kept me from total despair and complete insanity: 1) having a foundation rooted in a Christian upbringing; 2) having a PRAYING family; and 3) having *The Spiritual Principles of 12 Step* programs such as Alcoholics Anonymous. Ultimately it was God's grace and loving mercy that kept me through it all; however, these three components mentioned above were instrumental to say the least. Many of the sayings, slogans, and proverbs referenced in the pages of this book will be familiar to some who have experienced the "ROOMS". Some of the jargon and terminology within this book is often used during 12 step meetings.

What makes this book different than some of the other recovery meditation books is the biblical and scriptural integration. Many of the *12* Step programs utilize spiritual principles derived from scripture. However, many of the literature and language used in these programs do not directly refer to scriptures or the God of Scriptures. As a Christian Addictions Counselor and one that is very acquainted with the recovery process, I find there is no substitute for the power of prayer and scripture. It is my prayer and hope that this book will find its way into the hands of those in need, be it in a group setting or in the hands of an individual who is new to recovery.

I write from a Christian worldview because my serenity, recovery and salvation all depend on my Higher Power who is the Lord Jesus Christ. Another reason I wrote this book is for believers who are in recovery. God revealed to me early in my recovery that He does not heal and deliver every addict identically. Some have instantaneous and miraculous manifestations of deliverance.  For others, the *process* of recovery is just as miraculous and amazing. Being a Christian and being in recovery is not in conflict. We go and grow in the recovery process. We go from faith to faith, from strength to strength and from glory to glory.

As a final thought, not 'using' is a giant step in the right direction. Many of us spent years attempting to get clean and stay clean. Some have died in their addiction while others are in institutions right now; perhaps even reading this book. It is my prayer that wherever this book finds you, it will be a tool that can be used to help you in your recovery process. I pray that it will help you to experience being CLEAN and SERENE.  Whatever state you are in at this present time, do not be discouraged. Don't give up!  And no matter what, DON'T PICK UP!!!

Instead, as the Apostle Peter wrote, "...continue to grow in the grace and knowledge of our Lord and Savior Jesus, the Messiah. Glory belongs to Him both now and on that eternal day! Amen." (2Peter 3:18 ISV)

Pages 101-107 of this book contain weapons and tools you can use in this battle against addiction. Please refer to these pages often; they may very well be the most powerful pages in this book.

## TRUE PEACE

### Daily Passage: Philippians 4:7

*And the peace of God, which passes all understanding, shall keep your hearts and minds through Christ Jesus*

During our addiction we very rarely, if ever experience true peace. Even when we got momentary relief from getting our fix it was short lived. We soon found ourselves on another mission. It is surprising that many who survive active addiction are not suffering from PTSD. We were often in hazardous and dangerous environments. We may have had to go into literal war zones to get our drugs. We worried about getting robbed or worse each time we went to certain places. Some of us barely escaped some of the situations we put ourselves in. We constantly had to look over our backs and sleep with one eye open. This is how we survived. We lived in a constant state of fear, uncertainty, and mayhem.

Today our desire is to live clean and serene. Being sober is fantastic but we desire serenity. We have endured the battle and came away with the battle scars as proof. In recovery we find peace by trusting in God. We cast our cares upon Him. We keep our minds focused on His will for us. As we do these things we experience a peace like never before. Things may not be going as planned today. We may have all manner of obstacles and trials facing us.

We may even have to deal with the wreckage of our past. But in the midst of these things we have a peace that most cannot understand. We know deep down that God will work things out for our good. No matter what our circumstances tell us, we trust God. This is true serenity. This is living clean and serene.

## Daily meditation

Today regardless of what my circumstances say, I will trust God. I will enjoy the peace that surpasses all understanding.

## Daily Prayer

God help me to rest in the peace You have provided for those who trust You. My prayer is to live clean and serene. Amen.

## Daily Reflections

# DARE TO DREAM

## Daily Passage: Proverbs 13:12a

*Hope deferred makes the heart sick*

One of the last things addiction takes from people is hope. Some have tried time and time again to stop and stay stopped only to relapse. Others have burned so many bridges that they fear going back. Addiction has a way of beating a person down to a point of despair, depression and utter hopelessness. Shame and guilt can compound this feeling of hopelessness. Many have lost a desire to live once they believe all hoped has gone. This is one of the most dangerous aspects of addiction.

Today if you have breath in your body then you still have hope. It does not matter if you are only one day into your recovery, if you don't pick up there is still hope for you. The only thing that will certainly make matters worse is *using*. Regardless of how dire the situation may seem, in no scenario is using a good choice. Each day that you say no to the urge to use you are triumphant. With each triumph your future grows brighter. Somewhere along the way we begin to hope again, dream again, and aspire once again. While we face many difficult obstacles in recovery, we do not face them without hope.

## Daily meditation

I am grateful for the hope I have today in recovery.
I will dream again!  Aspire again! And I will live
again!

## Daily Prayer

God, renew my hope today as I meditate on Your
goodness and the blessings of recovery.  Amen.

# Daily Reflections

## WORTHY OF TRUST

### Daily Passage: Isaiah 40:13

*But those who hope in the LORD will renew their strength. They will soar on wings like eagles; they will run and not grow weary, they will walk and not be faint*

Letting go and letting God requires that we trust that He has our best interest at heart. Many times while in our addiction it was only by the grace of God that we lived to see another day. Now that we have begun to live sober, we experience moments of clarity. During these times we reflect on the many occasions that a loving God intervened on our behalf. The more that is revealed the easier it becomes to trust and hope in God. In essence God has given cause to hope by faithfully loving us when we were hell-bent on self-destruction.

Today this same loving God is with us in the process of recovery. His desire is that we live and have abundant lives. We will not face the challenges of life alone. The same God that kept us from dangers seen and unseen during our active addiction has not forsaken us during our recovery. When we are weak He will strengthen us. Regardless of what we face today, let us be encouraged that we are never alone.

## Daily meditation

Today I will be encouraged by the fact that a Loving God has my best interest at heart. If He cared for me during active addiction, will He not continue to care for me in recovery?

## Daily Prayer

God help me to be more aware of the love and care you extend to me on a daily basis. Don't let me be discouraged with well doing. Amen

## Daily Reflections

# TRUE GRIT

## Daily Passage: Galatians 6:9

*Let us not become weary in doing good, for at the proper time we will reap a harvest if we do not give up.*

For many of us it became very difficult to find ways and means to continue feeding our addiction. We did many things we told ourselves we would never do. The day in and day out methods we had to come up with to get and use our substance became tedious and tiresome. We subjected ourselves to degrading and compromising situations only to reap a reward that left us unfulfilled. Sadly when we were caught in the grips of active addiction we did not give up when we grew disenchanted with the things we had to do to get a fix.

Today we must use that same tenacity and grit in our recovery. The same way we chased that next high we must chase after recovery. We are doing what God desires today. We are respecting our temples and renewing our mindsets. We are on a good and righteous path. Regardless of the hurdles life throws our way today we must keep our eyes on the prize. Continue to seek a closer relationship with God. Continue to pray even if it feels like it is not working. Keep doing the next right thing for the right reasons. God will reward you more than you can imagine.

## Daily meditation

Today my recovery is my main priority. I will pursue recovery as hard as I did my drug of choice in active addiction.

## Daily Prayer

God grant me the strength to grind and work as hard at my recovery as I did to get my fix. Help me to overcome every adversity and roadblock to my recovery. Amen

# Daily Reflections

## LIAR, LIAR

### Daily Passage: 1 Corinthians 3:18

*Stop deceiving yourselves. If you think you are wise by this world's standards, you need to become a fool to be truly wise.*

In active addiction we became masters of manipulation. We had to quickly learn the art of deception to maintain our cover stories and excuses for our actions. At some point we became so good at lying that we even fooled ourselves. It has been said that some of the best liars are those who believe their own lie. We had to convince others that our lives were not unmanageable. We had to come up with reasons why we did not fulfill our obligations and responsibilities. We became gifted at justifying and rationalizing all types of things. Finding angles, loop holes, and exploits were a means to an end for us.

Today it is vital that we avoid such a mindset. What served us once as a survival skill during our active addiction will not serve us well in recovery. Many have entered rehab or programs for substance abuse with the same mentality they relied on when they were using. It is very difficult and nearly impossible for such a person to receive the help being offered. In the process of trying to outwit our counselors, therapists, and physicians we unwittingly doom ourselves to failure. Our way did not work. What we did got us here in need of help. It is time we give ourselves a chance by humbling ourselves, getting honest, and accepting the help in front of us.

## Daily meditation

Today I will be honest with self and accept that I don't know it all. I will accept the help made available to me.

## Daily Prayer

God help me not to fight my help today. Increase my ability to be honest with myself and others. Amen

# Daily Reflections

# SOMETHING DIFFERENT FOR A CHANGE

## Daily Passage: Proverbs 1:15

*My son, do not follow them in their way. Do not even set foot on their path.*

During our active addiction many of us had our favorite people, places, and things that were associated with that lifestyle. It may have been your favorite cousin you got high with. It may have been a favorite drinking buddy. Some of us had our trusted spots we knew we could always count on to go get high. There were certain things we did that we only did because we knew it was a means to get our fix.

Today we are trying to do something different for a change. It is often during these times that we are visited by or run into people from our days of active addiction. They may invite you to come to an old 'playground' with old 'playmates'. Our recovery must come first today. Going backwards is not an option. The path many of us escaped by the grace of God was one that led to death and destruction. As enticing as the offer to return or revisit these old 'playgrounds and playmates' is, it could be the worst decision you may ever make. Many have relapsed having been lured away from the new path of recovery by playmates from the days of active addiction.

## Daily meditation

Today I will stay the course and avoid going backwards regardless of how enticing it may be.

## Daily Prayer

God give me the courage to say No and stick to my guns. Help me to see possible triggers to relapse and to avoid them. Amen

# Daily Reflections

# TRUTH BE TOLD

## Daily Passage: Proverbs 1:30

*They refused my advice. They despised my every warning.*

Who loves being told what to do? When we were using, we did not like to be bothered. We despised and feared being confronted or corrected by others. For this reason we often avoided certain people. Maybe it was a concerned parent, teacher, or guardian.  We may have found ourselves hiding out in our own home if a loved one came knocking on the door to check on us. We grew tired of everyone "trying to tell us how to live our lives". Some of us went to great lengths to avoid the people we knew that would have "something to say" about what we were doing.

Today in recovery we cannot afford to think like this. We have to be open-minded and willing to accept those who are in our lives to help assist us on this journey. Sometimes this may include having to be confronted on things we do that are detrimental to our progress.  Changing our outlook on how people show concern for us can go a long way. If we see that people have a genuine concern for us and our wellbeing, it makes it easier to accept their help. Taking the suggestions and heeding the warnings of those who are here to help us in our recovery increases our chances of staying clean and sober.

## Daily meditation

Today I will take suggestions from those who genuinely care about me and be willing to take a look at my actions.

## Daily Prayer

God give me the wisdom to know when people are truly in my corner. Keep me from jumping to conclusions based in fear or pride. Amen

# Daily Reflections

# NOT SO HAPPY ENDING

## Daily Passage: Proverbs 2:11

*Foresight will protect you. Understanding will guard you.*

Many of us tried desperately to 'use' successfully, to no avail. Most of us have come to the conclusion that it is impossible for us to ever 'use' successfully. We have exhausted every known way to attempt to 'use' without suffering the consequences that inevitably followed after each failed attempt. We even tried methods such as moderation and replacing our drug of choice. Each time, the results were always the same. We ended up caught again in the same vicious cycle of addiction and often in a worst predicament. The old adage for an alcoholic or addict is "One is too many and a thousand is never enough" (Author Unknown). This has proven to be true in my case time and time again.

Today, armed with such knowledge and understanding, we stand a chance against the faulty thinking patterns associated with addiction. Often, during our recovery, we will have to deal with thoughts that challenge what we have come to believe. It is not abnormal for the addict in recovery to think about the 'good times' during active addiction. But if we allow that movie to play out in our mind it always ended the same. Remembering what it was like at the end of our road can be helpful during these times. Remembering how addiction beat us to a pulp can go a long way towards shattering the illusion of the 'good times'.

**Daily meditation**

Today I understand that I can never 'use' successfully. I will not fall victim to having selective memory.

**Daily Prayer**

God enable me to recognize unhealthy thinking. Help me to keep in remembrance how using destroyed my quality of life, stole my peace and nearly cost me my life.  Amen

# Daily Reflections

## A NEW PATH

### Daily Passage: Proverbs 3:5

*Trust the LORD with all your heart, and do not rely on your own understanding.*

During our time of active addiction trust was hard to come by. Many of us found out the hard way that people will lie and connive to get what they want. This is especially true in the subculture we had become accustomed with. We learned very soon not to send a fellow addict with our money to buy anything, especially not drugs. If we did, we would be lucky to only have them skim off some for themselves. We ourselves may have pinched a little off here and there when no one was looking. In such an environment it is very hard to trust or even be trusted. For many involved in this lifestyle these things are understood and common knowledge.

Today we have to learn to operate by a new set of principles. The lack of trust we had to adopt to protect ourselves in active addiction is not beneficial for us now. It is necessary that we trust God in this process. He is able to direct our path and keep us from falling back in the quick sand of addiction. There are many things about this new way of life that we have yet come to understand. This is why God has placed people in our lives at this time to help us along. Even if you have not gotten to the point in your recovery that you can trust people, it is not abnormal. However, it is extremely important to trust God and know that He has you covered. Part of trusting Him is allowing those He sends to help you to accomplish the assignment given to them.

**Daily meditation**

Today I don't have to understand the entire process. All I have to do is trust that God knows what He is doing.

**Daily Prayer**

God I trust you. I acknowledge You in all my ways. Please direct my paths.  Amen

# Daily Reflections

## HE INSIDE JOB

### Daily Passage: Proverbs 4:23

*Guard your heart more than anything else, because the source of your life flows from it.*

As we get more clean time certain things become more apparent. Having years of sobriety does not equate to years of recovery. Many have found that after putting down the drug or substance they still find their lives chaotic or drama filled. It's as if somewhere along the way we come to find that drugs were not the only problem. Now we no longer have drugs to blame for situations we got ourselves in, ruining relationships and making bad decisions. For some this is a rude awakening. We have to accept that putting down the drugs was only a GIGANTIC step in the right direction.

Today we understand that abstinence alone does not equal recovery. It is often said that recovery is an inside job. While we must not ever use drugs or alcohol it is equally important that we do some work in recovery. Most of the real work is inward in nature. Changing people, places, and things can be useless if we don't change ourselves. Many people are mistaken when they equate outward blessings of sobriety with recovery. As we stop using we are able to gain things. We may get a good paying job, new clothes, car or home. None of these things mean we have begun to work on the deep-seated issues that are underneath the surface. Remember, we became very good at wearing masks in our active addiction. Getting to the root of our issues will require that we become willing to go to the heart of the matter.

**Daily meditation**

Today I will be willing to go beyond the superficial. I don't just want to be sober. I want to recover.

**Daily Prayer**

God reveal the things I need to work on to truly recover. Expose anything in my heart and mind that will hinder me from growth in this process. Amen

# Daily Reflections

## THEY MAY HAVE A POINT

### Daily Passage: Proverbs 5:12

*Oh, how I hated discipline! How my heart despised correction!*

When we were in active addiction many of us did what we wanted and answered to no one. The only thing we obeyed was the urge to get and 'use' more. We did not enjoy anything that restricted our ability to get a fix when we needed it. For this reason many of us found ourselves without a job, relationship, and place to live. These things all have somethings in common. All of these things require self-control and discipline. It takes a certain level of self-discipline to show up to work and preform your duties. Employers expect an employee to work in a structured environment and follow a certain set of regulations. Being held to these standards can be difficult for someone in the grips of the obsessive and compulsive nature of addiction. Many of our relationships suffered because we despised being shown the error of our ways.

Today we can accept constructive criticism. This is especially true when we know it is coming from a person who genuinely cares for our wellbeing. We understand that we need structure and discipline in our lives. Those who are in place to help us achieve our goals in recovery are not our enemies. We can receive what they have to say because we know they mean me no harm. Today I am willing to take suggestions even if it means making changes. God uses people in our lives to help us grow in this process. Today I am willing to be open to the possibility that I may be wrong.

**Daily meditation**

Today I am grateful that there are people in my life who care enough to confront me when I stray from the path or get out of line.

**Daily Prayer**

God help me not to despise Your correction. Enable me to discern when people are trying to help me. Amen

# Daily Reflections

# PLAYING WITH FIRE

## Daily Passage: Proverbs 6:27-28

*Can you carry fire against your chest without burning your clothes? Can you walk on hot coals without burning your feet?*

Living clean and sober can be liberating and give us a new vigor for life. Sometimes we began to consider how others we 'used' with could benefit from this new way of living. We begin to convince ourselves that we should go back into our old stomping grounds and pull them out of the muck and mire. This is a noble idea but can be a disaster. While we may have a daily reprieve from the obsession and compulsion to 'use' it does not mean we are invincible. No matter how long we are clean and sober we are never immune to the temptation to 'use' again. This does not mean we live in fear. It does, however, mean we must use wisdom. This means avoiding putting ourselves in situations from which we may not come out of clean and sober.

Today, we know the joys and freedom of recovery. Our lives are much better since we stopped using. We want others to know that there is a better way to live. However, letting others know cannot come at the expense of our own sobriety.  For instance, a recovering crack addict has no business going back into an old crack house in attempts to show off their new found recovery. A recovering alcoholic should not decide to show up at Happy Hour attempting to describe how happy they are about living sober. This is equivalent to playing with fire. More often than not the person in recovery will get burned in such a situation. Good intentions cannot be a substitute for wisdom. Again, we must **NEVER** back ourselves in a corner that we cannot come out of clean and sober.

## Daily meditation

Today I will not allow my good intentions to negatively impact my recovery. I will use wisdom and common sense in all my affairs.

## Daily Prayer

God help me to do the right things for the right reasons. Help me to walk wisely and keep me from the paths that would cause me to slip, stumble, and/or fall. Amen

# Daily Reflections

# TIMING IS EVERYTHING

## Daily Passage: Matthew 10:16

*Therefore, be wise as serpents, and harmless as doves.*

Making amends is a part of the process of recovery. During active addiction we did great harm not only to ourselves but to those around us. Anyone in the wake of our destructive tendencies would fall victim to our actions and self-centeredness. When we were caught up in the grips of our addiction we were like Dr. Jekyll and Mr. Hyde. When Mr. Hyde took over we became oblivious to the feelings of others around us. The only thing that mattered to us was where we would get our next 'one'. This behavior left a trail of destruction and damaged relationships. As we get some clean time and a little sobriety under our belts, it may be tempting to try to prematurely make amends. This is not wise. If we are patient, in due time, opportunities will arise for amends to be made. But we must be careful not to do more harm in an effort to feel better about ourselves.

Today we are on the right path. We are living our lives without the use of any mind altering or mood altering substances. This is a great feeling. We are starting to see the benefits of sobriety and clean living. We want those from our past to see we are healthier now. We want them to see the progress we have made. We also want to make amends whenever possible. However there is a time and place for everything and we must use wisdom when making amends. Sometimes those we have harmed will not be in a place to receive our attempt to make amends. We have to understand that, at times, approaching such a person could do more harm to both parties. And for the love of God, NEVER try to make amends to a drug dealer you stole from. In due season, God will open the doors for amends to be made during our process of recovery. Until then the best amends we can make is to stay clean and not repeat our same old behaviors.

**Daily meditation**

Today I will allow God to open doors so I can make amends. I will be patient during my process.

**Daily Prayer**

God help me to be wise as a serpent yet harmless as a dove. Let my actions be led by You and not my self-centeredness.

# Daily Reflections

# WAIT FOR IT....

## Daily Passage: Ecclesiastes 3:1

*There is an appointed time for everything. And there is a time for every event under heaven-.*

During our active addiction instant self-gratification was at the center of our way of living. We had to have it yesterday. We could not get our drug of choice fast enough. We did many things we hate to even admit just to get that fix. Whenever the obsession and compulsion hit us we needed that next hit or next drink right then not later. We tried various delivery methods that we figured would give us the quickest feeling of euphoria. If we did not have money at the time we manipulated whomever we could to get what we wanted. If that didn't work we would resort to lying, stealing, or doing whatever it took to appease that urge to get high. Our cravings ruled us. Our urges were king. We were on a mission to get that quick fix.

Today in recovery it may be difficult to allow things just to unfold. Having had a good portion of our lives devoted to chasing instant self-gratification, conditioned us not to wait. This behavior and mindset is counter-productive at this phase of our lives. It's one of the many survival skills we used during active addiction, which has outlived its usefulness. Today we have turned our will and our lives over to the care of a loving God. We have asked Him to order our steps. We have begun to trust Him. We have begun to see Him supply our every need. However, there are things we still desire. There are things that we want to take place. We have started to dream again and even make plans. It is very important that we stay out of God's way. We must remember that He knows best. He withholds some of our desires from us until we are equipped to handle them because He loves us.

## Daily meditation

Today I will not be discouraged if one door shuts because I know in whom I have put my trust.

## Daily Prayer

God, help me to see Your loving hand at work in my life. Keep me from getting ahead of Your plans for me.

# Daily Reflections

# MATURATION

## Daily Passage: 1 Corinthians 13:11

*When I was a child, I talked like a child; I thought like a child, I reasoned like a child. When I became a man, I put the ways of childhood behind me.*

Self-centeredness is at the core of addiction. During our active addiction it was all about us. We were focused on finding ways and means to get what we needed at whatever cost. If it cost us a relationship we didn't care as long as we got what we needed at the time. If it cost us our dignity, that mattered little to us as long as we got what we wanted in the process. We would say or do just about anything for the 'next one'. We lashed out verbally at those who would try to talk us out of our behavior. Some of us threw tantrums and became destructive when we could not get loved ones to enable us. If we had to choose between our responsibilities and getting the 'next one,' we shucked our duties.

Today our mindset is very different. We consider those around us. We consider their feelings and needs. It takes work and time but we are becoming dedicated to change and recovery. This can be difficult because we are behaving as responsible individuals. We are trying to communicate in a mature and respectful manner. Our goals have changed. We no longer just want what is best for us. We are concerned with how our actions affect others in our lives. Our level of maturity is in direct correlation to the amount of work we are willing to put into our recovery. We have to remember that there are things we have to do in recovery that may not feel good. There will be times we do the right thing just because it is the right thing to do. These are all signs of growth. As we grow in grace we have to remember it is a process.

## Daily meditation

Today I will put into practice the principles I have been learning in my recovery. I will remember that sometimes the mature thing to do may be difficult and uncomfortable.

## Daily Prayer

God, thank you for the grace you have given us to grow and make mistakes in this process. Help me to do the things that are pleasing in Your sight.

# Daily Reflections

## GROW IN GRACE

### Daily Passage: 2 Peter 3:18

*But be always growing in the grace and knowledge of our Lord and Saviour Jesus Christ. To Him be all glory, both now and to the day of Eternity*

Shame and guilt plagued us when we were in active addiction. Many times when we sobered up long enough to reflect on what we did the night before and we could barely stand to look at ourselves in the mirror. Our only resort was to cling to the very thing that caused us the pain. In an effort to escape the shame and guilt we only compounded its effects. People who have not been caught in this vicious cycle have a hard time understanding what it is like. We beat ourselves up more than anyone could imagine. We cannot stand what we have become and doubt anyone would forgive us or understand. In fact, we find it hard to forgive ourselves and cannot understand why we do the things we hate.

Today it can be difficult to give ourselves a break. We are often more critical of ourselves than others. We may have yet to forgive ourselves for the things we did in our active addiction. The concept of grace may seem foreign to some of us. When we began to consider the amazing grace of God it is even more overwhelming and hard to conceptualize. The grace of God is unmerited. That means we cannot earn it by what we do right. It is God's gift to us because

He loves us unconditionally. So if it cannot be earned by good works, it cannot be lost *when* we mess up. Not IF we mess up, but *WHEN* we mess up or fall short.   At times, the hardest thing for a recovering addict to do is to forgive ourselves. We also have to be okay with the fact that no matter what we do, some of the people we have harmed will never be forgiving towards us. This is sad but true. Sometimes the things we have done to others during our addiction try to come back and haunt us. The memories of acts we committed may rear their ugly heads and try to shame us into a relapse. It is during these times, especially, that we must cling to the grace and forgiveness of God.  As we grow in grace we begin to become better at forgiving ourselves. But it may take some more time than others.

## Daily meditation

Today I will give myself a break. I will accept God's amazing grace. If God has forgiven me, who am I not to forgive myself?

## Daily Prayer

God grant me the ability to forgive myself. Do not let shame and guilt hold the same power over me that they once did. Let me walk in forgiveness and grace. Amen

# Daily Reflections

# FLATTERY GETS YOU NO WHERE

## Daily Passage: Proverbs 27:6

*Wounds from a sincere friend are better than many kisses from an enemy.*

During our active addiction we surrounded ourselves with people we knew would not try to discourage our 'using'. We avoided the people who would tell us the truth. Many times we already felt horrible about how far our addiction had taken us. For this very reason we flocked with birds of a feather. We did not have to worry about people in the shot house trying to do an intervention on us. We could be sure that other pot-heads were not going to say we needed to get help. Our drug dealers certainly were not going to tell us we were looking sick and needed to get off the stuff. In essence, we befriended those who meant us no good and kept at bay those who desired to see us well. This is part of the insanity of addiction. Addiction kept us isolated from our true friends. Even when we were aware that we were in bad company we overlooked it to get high.

Today we do not avoid being confronted by a sincere friend. We do not allow them to condemn us. We understand that we are growing in grace. However, we do welcome feedback from those who genuinely care for us. We are not running from correction today. We understand that we have to be made aware of things in order to grow. We may not like or even agree with what is presented. The evidence of growth is that today we are willing to honestly take a look at what is being conveyed. This is not to say another person's perception is our reality in all situations. It does mean we are open to the "wounds of a friend". Sometimes the truth hurts. Nevertheless the kisses of an enemy can be deadly.

## Daily meditation

Today I will allow people who care for me to point out things they see that I may not. Even if it hurts my ego I will take a look at it.

## Daily Prayer

God help me to remain open-minded and approachable. Give me strength today to make difficult adjustments and accept constructive criticism.

# Daily Reflections

# TAKE OFF THE MASK

## Daily Passage: Ecclesiastes 3:3

*There is a time to tear down and a time to build up.*

One of the things we became very good at during our active addiction is hiding. We spent a great deal of time building facades. We wore many masks when we were 'using'. It became hard for some of us to keep this up. Some of us forgot who we were at some point. We built up an image for certain situations and environments. These were coping mechanism and survival skills. It was what we felt we had to do to get what we needed. We did not want to stick out like a sore thumb. We wanted to be a "part of". Those who were a "part of" got passed the peace-pipe. So we adopted the saying, "when in Rome do as the Romans do". We adopted the lingo, mannerisms, and customs of those we were around.

When we embark on the journey of recovery it may be difficult not to revert back to learned behaviors. In recovery we are asked to unmask. We have to tear down facades. The images we portrayed no longer serve a purpose. It is time to "get real". This can be a long process. We used this as a defense mechanism at times. Feeling vulnerable or appearing weak in our old environments could mean becoming a victim. Today we are surrounding ourselves with those who are in recovery and people who desire to see us succeed. We gradually become willing to be ourselves. We don't have to hide. We are free to be who God created us to be. Flawed as we may be, it does not matter. We are peeling back the layers we built up in active addiction. We are a work in progress. We are not seeking the approval of others. We are practicing self-acceptance today.

**Daily meditation**

Today I don't have to wear a mask. I can be me. There is freedom in recovery. I am no longer bound by my addiction to be something I am not.

**Daily Prayer**

God give me the courage to take off the mask. Help me to tear down defenses that I built in fear. Let me walk in the freedom that has been given to me in recovery. Amen.

# Daily Reflections

## THE BEST POLICY

### Daily Passage: Colossians 3:9

*Do not lie to one another, since you have put away
[the conduct of] your old person with its practices.*

If you were like most of us, lying became second
nature during our active addiction. When we were
caught in the grips; many times we lost track of
tangled webs we weaved. Our deception was a tool
we used to get what we wanted. Sometimes we lied
so long that we began to believe our own
fabrications. Many addicts are habitual liars. This
means lying was a learned behavior that formed into
a habit or way of living. Point blank, we WERE
dishonest people in all our affairs.

In recovery, we will not go far if we are dishonest.
Dishonesty is counterproductive to our new way of
life. There is a saying, "Old habits die hard"
(Author Unknown). We often find this to be the
case in our recovery. We may be on the right track
but that does not mean we can stop being vigilant. If
we do not work on our underlying issues, old
patterns, and behaviors, we will find ourselves clean
but living dirty. Today it may be tempting to lie to
get our way but we have to fight the urge to be
dishonest. Today we must put into practice what we
have learned in our recovery. If we are unwilling to
put these new things into practice we will find
ourselves miserable unchanged sober people.

## Daily meditation

Today as tempting as it may be to practice dishonesty, I will not. Instead, to the best of my ability, I will be honest in all my affairs.

## Daily Prayer

God, give me the courage be honest today. Help me to strip away my old ways of lying and deceit because they serve no purpose in my life today. Amen.

# Daily Reflections

# NO ONE SIZE FITS ALL

## Daily Passage: Mark 5:26

*Although she had endured a great deal under the care of many doctors and had spent all of her money, she had not been helped at all, but rather grew worse.*

Many of us have tried to get clean in the past. We may have even had short periods of success. We may have been mandated or volunteered for treatment. We may have seen various medical professionals, counselors, and therapist. Many have even tried medication to help with substance abuse problems. It's not uncommon to hear the stories of other recovering addicts who have had relapse after relapse. Some of us have been in every type of rehab program known to man. This is not a badge of honor but a glimpse into the severity of our problem. There is a saying that, "some are sicker than others" (Author Unknown). This is often the case with addicts because it is common for us to have dual diagnosis. Having a dual diagnosis combined with the fact that addiction also affects us spiritually; it is no wonder why so many relapse.

In recovery you will often find that there is no one size fit all treatment. Some of us will need medication as a part of our Recovery and Treatment Plan. Some may need more intensive trauma counseling in addition to group therapy. However, there is one thing we must not overlook in this process. That one thing is the spiritual aspect of addiction and recovery. This is not the same as religion. Spirituality and religion do not always go hand and hand. A person can be religious and not have a connection or relationship with GOD. However, without God we cannot recover. Again, we may get clean and sober but that does not equal recovery. There are aspects that relate to addiction and recovery that only God can attend to. Medicine, therapy, and counseling all have their place in recovery. But none of these can take the place of God or do for us what He can.

**Daily meditation**

Today I will take matters to God that men cannot fix. I will trust God to renew my heart, mind, and spirit.

**Daily Prayer**

God I desire a genuine relationship with You. I need a relationship that will address the needs that only You can meet. Amen.

# Daily Reflections

## LET US THANK HIM

### Daily Passage: Ephesians 3:20

*Glory belongs to God, whose power is at work in us. By this power he can do infinitely more than we can ask or imagine.*

We have had some very dark days in our past. There were times we had almost lost all hope. Some of us experienced bouts of depression that made us consider ending it all. During these times we could not imagine getting free from the clutch of this beast called addiction. We felt the world would be better off without us. We had failed at living sober and were struggling at getting high. Then there came the point when the drugs or alcohol did nothing for us. We no longer got high but we still needed to 'use' just to feel normal. We felt helpless and unable to change our situation. We had become a slave to our addiction. Some of us lost friends to addiction but that did not stop us. Some of us overdosed and nearly died ourselves. It seemed nothing would stop us except the grave.

Today, by the grace of God, we have a newfound outlook on life in recovery. We have seen God work miracles in our lives. Each day that we are given a reprieve from the compulsion and desire to 'use' is a miracle and a blessing. Some of us have begun to get things back that we lost. Some regain the respect of family members, restored relationships, and even material things. Jobs, homes, and reconciled relationships are just a few of the things many have experienced in recovery. However, the longer we stay the course the more God's grace amazes us. He gives us the desires of our hearts and blesses us immeasurably. There are days we look over our lives and tear up as we consider what God has done. This is even more heartfelt when we consider that at one point all we desired and asked for was to be set free.

## Daily meditation

Today I will take a moment to consider where God has brought me from. I will give Him thanks for His grace, which is truly amazing.

## Daily Prayer

God, today I have no request and no petition. I only offer to You my thanksgiving for all You have done in my life. My attitude is one of gratitude. Amen.

# Daily Reflections

# NO TIME FOR FOOLISHNESS

## Daily Passage: Psalm 34:14

*Turn away from evil and do good. Search for peace, and work to maintain it.*

During our days in active addiction there was always some type of drama going on. Our days were filled with chaos and all the drama involved with getting high. We saw people beat up for coming up short or trying to skim and 'pinch'. We may have seen people robbed, maimed, or worse. Almost every day, we would hear about 'so and so' getting busted for selling drugs. Some of the people we ran with would get picked up for stealing to support their addiction. Some of us became addicted to the drama as much as we were to our drug of choice. The place where most of the illicit and illegal actions took place is where we gravitated towards. Our search for the next high led us into some of the most dangerous and volatile places. Nevertheless, to maintain our high we would often revisit these places even at our own risk and regardless of the foolishness we had to endure.

In recovery, we may find that we still have a pull toward drama. We often find that some of us even stir up things for no good reason. We come to find out that not everyone in our circle of recovery is trying to change. There may be some who still have the need to cause commotions and stir up strife. We have to decide that this is not what we want in our lives today. We have to care enough about our recovery to protect it from those who could care less. We must pursue peace and do the right thing today. While we may have grown accustomed to riotous living; today we seek serenity. It is completely fine to remove ourselves from circles that become toxic and unhealthy. This is what being responsible looks like.

## Daily meditation

Today I will not take part in the drama. I am about my recovery. I don't have time for foolishness. My recovery takes priority.

## Daily Prayer

God, give me the strength and fortitude to extract myself from situations and surroundings that would do me harm. Help me to maintain peace and shun drama. Amen.

# Daily Reflections

## WHEN THE TRUTH HURTS

### Daily Passage: Proverbs 14:12

*There is a way which seemeth right unto a man, but the ends thereof are the ways of death.*

No one could tell us anything when were in full blown active addiction. We knew better than anyone who tried to tell us we were heading down the wrong path. Sometimes we may have known they were not completely wrong but we were going to stick to our guns. Even when a person spoke from experience, we had an answer or rebuttal. One of our favorite lines were, "that's them not me". We would argue that just because something happened to you it did not mean the same held true for us. Later we found that we did, indeed, wind up in some very bad predicaments. Many of our worst memories can be traced back to our ego, pride, and rebellion.

Today we cannot afford to let our ego stand in the way of our recovery. We come to understand that we do not have all the answers early in recovery. This remains true no matter how long we have been sober. Sometimes someone on the outside looking in can see what we fail to see. We may need to consider what others make us aware of even if it does not sit well with us. God places people in our lives to assist in the healing process. Sometimes these people aggravate us because we know; deep down inside that they are speaking the truth. We have the ability to convince ourselves of just about anything if it involves getting what we want. Therefore, it is imperative that we don't ignore the warnings God gives us through the people He places in our lives. This may seem to be a redundant principle of the recovery process. However, those who grab ahold of this concept greatly increase their chances of staying clean and serene.

## Daily meditation

Today I will not be quick to discount what others have brought to my attention. I will truly consider what they are saying because it could be life-saving information.

## Daily Prayer

God help me to be open-minded today. I do not want to let my pride cause me to fall. Amen.

# Daily Reflections

## IT'S NOT LUCK, ITS FAVOR

### Daily Passage: Romans 8:28

*And we know that for those who love God all things work together for good, for those who are called according to his purpose.*

Murphy's Law is the old adage that states: "Anything that can go wrong will go wrong" (Author Unknown). Some of us felt this way during our active addiction. It seemed like we hit obstacles at every corner while trying to get high. Sometimes we resorted to unthinkable acts when all else failed. There have been many who resorted to prostituting themselves only to be rewarded with "dummies" or fake drugs. Imagine degrading yourself because you could not get the money any other way only to be paid in baking soda instead of cocaine. Some of us don't have to imagine because it happened to us. We begged, borrowed and scraped just to be sold oregano instead of marijuana. Some are in jail or in the grave because the quest to get high went tragically wrong.

Today we do not have to live under the fear of impending doom. We are not cursed. No, in fact we have been blessed to walk in our recovery. To be in the land of the living is a gift of God. It is a gift, that if considered closely will leave us in amazement. Think of all the times things could have horribly gone wrong, then factor in the dangers seen and unseen that we lived through. It is a miracle that many of us are alive today. How many things had to work in our favor to get to this point in our recovery?

## Daily meditation

Today I will consider how God has and continues to work all things together for my good.

## Daily Prayer

God, I will not fear what lies ahead or around the corner. You have continued to prove Your love for me time after time. Thank you for Your favor, Amen.

# Daily Reflections

# RECOVERY IS NOT A 2O YARD DASH

## Daily Passage: Ecclesiastes 9:11b

*The fastest runner doesn't always win the race, and the strongest warrior doesn't always win the battle.*

One of our main objectives during active addictions was to get our hands on our drug of choice as soon as possible. This often meant we needed to make a 'quick buck' or 'fast money'. We worked angles and look for the paths of least resistance. We did not learn patience during our active addiction. We became conditioned to move with haste when we began to 'jones' or crave for our fix. In a sense, when the urge hit we were off to the races. We were like greyhounds chasing our drug around the track trying to get it before the next addict. We had to beat out anyone who stood in our way. We played foul and fought dirty. This is what we did to get a quick fix.

Recovery is not a race. We are not in competition with others in recovery. It is unhealthy to compare our progress with that of others. We all recover at different rates. The most important thing is to stay the course and do not look back. While recovery is not a race we must have endurance like a marathon runner. Things will not happen overnight. We have to stick and stay. We have to stick to path of recovery and stay with the winners. The winners are those who are in recovery and practicing a new way of life. We need these people in our lives because recovery is a battle. We will often need help no matter how strong we think we are. Sometimes we show the most strength when we are strong enough to ask for help. This requires a new way of thinking. We cannot see these people as competition or threats. That is called "stinking thinking" and it will most certainly cause us stumble.

## Daily meditation

Today I will not be out for only myself. I will not compare myself to others. I will ask for help.

## Daily Prayer

God help me to shed old ways of thinking that I learned as survival skills during my addiction. Amen.

# Daily Reflections

# ONE IS TOO MANY

## Daily Passage: Proverbs 23:31-35

*Do not gaze at wine when it is red, when it sparkles in the cup, when it goes down smoothly! In the end it bites like a snake and poisons like a viper. Your eyes will see strange sights, and your mind will imagine confusing things. You will be like one sleeping on the high seas, lying on top of the rigging. "They hit me," you will say, "but I'm not hurt! They beat me, but I don't feel it! When will I wake up so I can find another drink?"*

Who among us has not woke up the next morning covered in bruises? Some of us have had many blackouts and cannot remember what we did the night before. People may come and tell us what we did but we do not recall the events. All we knew for certain is that we were sore and hung over. Sadly most of us lived by the expression "the hair of the dog that bit you" (Author Unknown). We would often act like the person described in the proverb above. The proverb goes, "They hit me," you will say, "but I'm not hurt! They beat me, but I don't feel it! When will I wake up so I can find another drink?" We awoke from a night of being abused by our addiction only to run right back to our abuser. This is the insanity of addiction.

In recovery, we are being gradually restored to sanity. As we do the work we get better. Doing the work does not make us immune to the temptation of going backwards. We have to remain determined and steadfast in our recovery. There will be days when it would seem that going back is not a bad idea. There will be days when we are tempted to just 'try one'. No matter how enticing it may look we must remember how it was at the end of the road. The addiction will conveniently leave out the horrible memories of our past. We have to remind ourselves that it would be insane to think we can ever 'use' successfully. Regardless of how good of an idea it may seem at the time, 'using' is NEVER the answer.

## Daily meditation

Today I will remember what my addiction took me through when I have the urge to go back. No matter how tempted I am, 'using' is **not** an option.

## Daily Prayer

God bring to remembrance those things I need to remember when I am tempted to go backwards. Help me to not sabotage my own recovery. Amen.

# Daily Reflections

## BIG 'I' LITTLE "u"

**Daily Passage: 2 Corinthians 10:12**

*We do not dare to classify or compare ourselves with some who commend themselves. When they measure themselves by themselves and compare themselves with themselves, they are not wise.*

One of the addict's trump cards in active addiction is comparison. We often minimize our plight by comparing ourselves to those in worse predicaments. This gives us a false sense that we are 'ok'. We may not be so far gone as to think we are fine but we feel that there are people worse off. Comparison helps us to continue using under these faulty assumptions. We used this reasoning to justify self-destruction. We could be looking in the mirror at famished, skeletal, scab covered reflections of our former selves. Comparison will tell us we look bad but Johnny or Susie looks way worse.

Today we must avoid the trap of comparing ourselves to others. When we catch ourselves doing this we have to ask ourselves why. Often when it is time to make uncomfortable changes we resort to this defense mechanism. When we don't want to look at ourselves we look at others instead. We can find the faults of others and say we are better than them. This is pride. The root of comparison is pride. It requires us to think less of others and more highly of ourselves. In the end, it serves no purpose but to bolster or pump up our own egos. Humility is having a healthy knowledge of one's self. We have to be willing to accept, acknowledge and work on our own shortcomings. Comparing ourselves to others is not only unwise but detrimental to our recovery.

## Daily meditation

Today I will practice humility. I will not think of myself as better than or less than anyone else.

## Daily Prayer

God, help me to understand humility. Let me see myself as you see me. Amen.

# Daily Reflections

# WORRYING IS WORISOME

## Daily Passage: Matthew 6:25

*Therefore I tell you, do not worry about your life, what you will eat or drink; or about your body, what you will wear. Is not life more than food and the body more than clothes?*

During our active addiction we worried about a great deal of things.  We worried about getting caught doing illegal things. We worried about being seen in places we were ashamed to be at. We worried what our loved ones thought of us. We worried about how our actions would affect our children. We worried if we would see another day. These worries took a backseat to our biggest worry of them all. We mainly worried that the sun would go down without us getting our next fix. We were more worried about getting our next one than anything else. This was what our life was centered around. We worried daily about acquiring, 'using', how to get more.

Now we enter recovery and are being taught to turn our will and our lives over to the care of God.  This can be very difficult to the most spiritual among us. It is not something we ever do perfectly at all times. However, it is something we must learn to practice daily. The cares of this world do not stop just because we get clean and sober! Just because we put down the substance will not eradicate having any concerns in life. Today we are not running from our responsibilities and we are trying to take better care of ourselves. We endeavor to live healthy and productive lives. One of the ways to live clean and serene is to trust the God we have turned our lives over to. This turning over of our lives is a daily and sometimes a moment-to-moment intentional act. When life begins to show up and the cares of this world threaten to shake us, we have to trust God. If we are completely honest, He has yet to fail us.

**Daily meditation**

Today my trust is in God. I will not believe He has brought me this far to leave me destitute and without hope.

**Daily Prayer**

God bring to my remembrance Your faithfulness. Remind me of all the times you were right on time. Help me to experience the serenity of resting in You. Amen.

## Daily Reflections

## CHILDLIKE FAITH

### Daily Passage: Matthew 18:3

*And he said: "Truly I tell you, unless you change and become like little children, you will never enter the kingdom of heaven.*

None of us were born knowing how to use drugs. We did not know how to roll a blunt, spliff, or joint the first time we tried. Neither did we know the different types of paraphernalia involved with using our later drugs of choice. We had to be taught how to '*use*'. Someone showed us the ropes. Someone showed you how to shoot up properly. Someone told you how to inhale. When those who were experienced in the lifestyle spoke, we listened. "Liquor before beer and you're in the clear" (Author Unknown) is not something a child knows. But most of us who were alcoholics learned that old saying early on along with many other sayings. We accepted these directions and suggestions with no questions asked; we were like trusting children when we first got started in our addiction. In essence we came into addiction as a child willing and trusting those who, in the end, were found to be untrustworthy.

How is it that we come into recovery defiant and unwilling to trust those who have our best interests at heart? We often come in kicking and screaming fighting our help. We swear we know better than those who have been in recovery long before us.

Many times we are unwilling to take their suggestions. This will not cut it. If we want to stick around and stay clean and sober we must become teachable. We cannot expect to live clean and serene if we are not. Understanding that we may know how to get high but know very little about staying clean will save us a lot of trouble. We have to be humble. It is important to realize those who have gone before us can save us from making the mistakes of many.

## Daily meditation

Today I will not be puffed up and prideful. I will listen to my predecessors and those living clean and serene.

## Daily Prayer

God help me become like a child again in this process of recovery. Help me to see how I was willing to listen to people who caused me harm but at times refuse to listen to those who now mean me well. Amen.

# Daily Reflections

# THE FOG IS LIFTED

## Daily Passage: John 10:10

*The thief comes only to steal, slaughter, and destroy. I've come that they may have life, and have it abundantly.*

It has been said that addiction is cunning, baffling, and powerful. Very similar to the passage above; addiction is a thief. Many can attest to being left penniless, jobless, and even homeless as a result of addiction. However, the material losses can pale in comparison to how addiction robs us of our dignity and hope. Those who have been caught in its grips can understand how cruel addiction can be. Ambitions, goals, and dreams we once had were stolen and replaced with fear, despair, and resentment.

Once we begin our new journey for recovery, many things become restored. As the fog begins to clear, we start to see the addiction for what it really is. We are no longer under the impression or illusion that the drugs or alcohol is our friend. Addiction has made it clear, its intent is to steal, kill, and destroy. So one day at a time we choose life. It is only by the grace of God that hope is restored during this process we call recovery.

## Daily meditation

I am grateful today for the awareness I have concerning addiction. I thank God for the restoration process of recovery.

## Daily Prayer

God help me this day to not be discouraged by the things I have lost due to addiction. But help me to rejoice in hope during this process of restoration. Amen.

# Daily Reflections

# The 12 Steps in Relation to Scripture

**Step 1: We admitted we were powerless over our addictions and compulsive behavior; that our lives had become unmanageable.**

*I know that nothing good lives in me, that is, in my sinful nature. For I have the desire to do what is good, but I cannot carry it out.* Romans 7:18

**Step 2: We came to believe that a power greater than ourselves could restore us to sanity.**

*For it is God who is at work in you to will and to act according to his good purpose.* Philippians 2:13

**Step 3: We made a decision to turn our life and our will over to the care of God.**

*Therefore, I urge you, brothers, in view of God's mercy, to offer your bodies as living sacrifices, holy and pleasing to God—this is your spiritual act of worship.* Romans 12:1

**Step 4: We made a searching and fearless moral inventory of ourselves.**

*Let us examine our ways and test them, and let us return to the LORD.* Lamentations 3:40

**Step 5: We admitted to God, to ourselves, and to another human being, the exact nature of our wrongs.**

*Therefore, confess your sins to each other, and pray for each other, so that you may be healed.*
James 5:16a

**Step 6: We were entirely ready to have God remove all these defects of character.**

*Humble yourselves before the Lord, and he will lift you up.* James 4:10

**Step 7: We humbly asked Him to remove all our shortcomings.**

*If we confess our sins, he is faithful and just and will forgive us our sins and purify us from all unrighteousness.* 1 John 1:9

**Step 8: We made a list of all persons we had harmed and became willing to make amends to them all.**

*"Do to others as you would have them do to you."* Luke 6:31

**Step 9: We made direct amends to such people whenever possible, except when to do so would injure them or others.**

*"Therefore, if you are offering your gift at the altar and there remember that your brother has something against you, leave your offering there in front of the altar. First go and be reconciled to your brother; and then come and offer your gift."* Matthew 5:23–24

**Step 10: We continued to take personal inventory and when we were wrong, promptly admitted it.**

*So, if you think you are standing firm, be careful that you don't fall!* 1 Corinthians 10:12

**Step 11: We sought through prayer and meditation to improve our conscious contact with God, praying only for knowledge of His will for us and the power to carry that out.**

*Let the word of Christ dwell in you richly.* Colossians 3:16a

**Step 12: Having had a spiritual experience as the result of these steps, we tried to carry this message to others, and practice these principles in all our affairs.**

*Brothers, if someone is caught in a sin, you who are spiritual should restore him gently. But watch yourself, or you also may be tempted.* Galatians 6:1

# THE COMPLETE SERENITY PRAYER

God grant me the serenity
To accept the things I cannot change;
Courage to change the things I can;
And wisdom to know the difference.

Living one day at a time;
Enjoying one moment at a time;
Accepting hardships as the pathway to peace;
Taking, as He did, this sinful world
As it is, not as I would have it;
Trusting that He will make all things right
If I surrender to His Will;
So that I may be reasonably happy in this life
And supremely happy with Him
Forever and ever in the next.
Amen.

# THE LORD'S PRAYER

Pray then like this:

'Our Father in heaven, hallowed be your name.

Your kingdom come, your will be done,

on earth as it is in heaven.

Give us this day our daily bread,

and forgive us our debts,

as we also have forgiven our debtors.

And lead us not into temptation,

but deliver us from evil.'

Matthew 6:9–13 (ESV) "

# MORE WILL BE REVEALED

## Last Words of Encouragement

Many of us have reached points during our journey when we are not sure if we can go on. During these times it may seem there is no way to deal or cope with the pain, confusion, or despair. We find ourselves in a situation where there seems to be no way out.

If you are able to read these words then THERE IS STILL HOPE for you. Every moment we have in this life is a gift from God. Though He may at times feel far away, know that He is near.

He has moved me to share with you that He has you covered. Do not give up or give in to the temptation to escape the present distress and discomfort. It is only temporary. Your next miracle will be right on time. Trust and believe in the One who has kept you by His grace and mercy. He cares for you and has worked things out in your favor already despite what your situation is telling you.

God has people in place to assist you. God has places to take you. He is not finished with you. Be encouraged. This, too, shall pass.

If today you feel overwhelmed, here is a passage that may shed some light on your current situation:

# 2 Kings 6:14-17 (ISV)

14) So the king of Aram sent out horses, chariots, and an elite force, and they arrived during the night and surrounded the city.

15) Meanwhile, the attendant to the man of God got up early in the morning and went outside, and there were the elite forces, surrounding the city, accompanied by horses and chariots! So Elisha's attendant cried out to him, "Oh no! Master! What will we do!?"

16) Elisha replied, "Stop being afraid, because there are more with us than with them!"

17) Then Elisha prayed, asking the Lord, "Please make him able to really see!" And so when the Lord enabled the young man to see, he looked, and there was the mountain, filled with horses and fiery chariots surrounding Elisha!